DATE DUE

DEC 27 1993		OCT 16 2001	
FEB 19 1994		MAY 3 2002	
		JAN 30 2007	
JUL 20 1994		JAN 25 2008	
FEB 25 1995			
APR 29 1995 JUN -7 1995			
AUG -7 1995			
SEP 29 1995			
JAN 13 1996			
JUN 15 1996			
OCT 10 1996			
JUN -8 1999			
NOV 27 1999			
MAR 10 2000			

Demco, Inc. 38-293

Netherlands

Donna Bailey

STECK-VAUGHN
L I B R A R Y
A Division of Steck-Vaughn Company

Hello! My name is Rien.

I live in Amsterdam, in the Netherlands.

I am going for a ride in the park on
my new green bike with Mom and Dad.

My little sister Anneke is too small to
ride a bike so Dad takes her on his bike.

We live on the corner of the street.

The bridge near our house goes over a canal.

We don't have room for a garden but

Mom grows flowers in the window boxes.

There are many canals in Amsterdam.
People have to be careful when
they park their car by a canal.
They don't want their car to roll
into the water.

Amsterdam is the capital of the Netherlands.
It is a very busy city.
Boats travel the canals and the river, and
there are many ships in the harbor.

Some of the bridges over the canals are
so low that boats cannot go under them.
Traffic must stop while the bridge
is raised to let the boats through.

Many people come into Amsterdam
every day to work.
The streets in the center of the city
are always full of cars and streetcars.

Some people leave their car
in a parking lot away from the city center.
Then they ride a streetcar or bus to work.
At one time people could borrow electric cars.
This was an experiment to cut down on
air pollution.

Many people ride bikes around the city.
Almost everyone has a bike so
sometimes there is a traffic jam of
bikes instead of cars!

Every morning I walk to school with my friends.
Our parents meet us after school.
I go home to have a snack and then
go to the park to ride my bike.

10

Sometimes I go to my friend's house
after school.

All three of us ride on his mom's bicycle.

I ride behind his mom and he rides
in front of her.

We usually play marbles or watch television.

In the winter, the canals in Amsterdam
often freeze.
If the ice is not too thin, people enjoy
skating along the frozen canals.

In the spring, we go to see the flowers
in the gardens at Keukenhof.
The gardens are filled with crocuses,
hyacinths, tulips, and daffodils.

13

On our way to Keukenhof, we pass
many bulb fields.
When the bulbs bloom, the bulb growers
cut off the heads of the flowers.
That keeps the flowers from using up
all the food stored in the bulbs.

When the leaves die, the growers
dig up the bulbs and send them to
the bulb market in Amsterdam.
They also send bulbs to countries
all over the world.

Thousands of flowers are used to
decorate floats for parades.
The stems of the flowers are
pushed into a wire framework.
Sometimes the framework is shaped
like an animal or a person.

16

During the summer, Dutch people often
go on bicycle trips.
The Netherlands is a good place
for a bicycle trip.
There are hundreds of cycling paths with
little bridges over the canals.

To find out what the Netherlands is like,
many tourists visit Madurodam.
The models at Madurodam show different
scenes of Dutch life.
All the towns, buildings, and people at
Madurodam are very small.

There are model ships, planes, and trains,
and even a model of Europort.
Europort is a big port in Rotterdam
on the southern coast.
It is the biggest and busiest port in Europe.

The land north of Amsterdam is very flat.
The lowest part of the province of North Holland
is 22 feet below the level of the North Sea.
A huge dike 18 miles long shuts off
the North Sea to make a shallow lake
called the IJsselmeer.

In this part of the country, pieces of
land called polders are separated
from each other by canals full of water.

Windmills pump the extra water from
the polders into the sea or a lake.
That is why there are so many windmills
in the Netherlands.

Many people sail boats
in the canals.
It sometimes looks strange when a boat
is moving through the fields!

There are many cows in North Holland, too.
The cows graze in the grassy pastures.
The grass is always green because
of all the water.

The cows give the farmers plenty of
milk and cream every day.
Many farmers use the milk to make
round Dutch cheeses.
Every Friday the farmers send their cheeses
to a market like Alkmaar.

Judges test the cheese before it is sold.
The judges make sure the cheese
is safe to eat.

The porters at Alkmaar carry the cheeses
on flat wooden trays.
The porters all wear white clothes.
The colored band on each porter's hat
shows which company the porter works for.

Before the big dike was built to make
the IJsselmeer, Marken was
a fishing village on an island.
Today it is part of North Holland and
is surrounded by polders.

The green, wooden houses in Marken
once stood on poles above the water.
Now the houses have brick cellars.
People in Marken wear traditional
costumes for special holidays,
such as the Queen's birthday.

On holidays, the girls wear
embroidered dresses with
red and white striped sleeves.
The men and boys wear
striped black and white shirts.

People living at Staphorst on
the other side of the IJsselmeer wear
their traditional costume all the time.
The women have colored shawls
and special caps.

In Staphorst, the children of each age group
wear a different costume.
This girl has an embroidered cap and dress.
Even the back wheel of her bicycle
has an embroidered cover.

Index

Editorial Consultant: Donna Bailey
Executive Editor: Elizabeth Strauss
Project Editor: Becky Ward

Picture research by Jennifer Garratt
Designed by Richard Garratt Design

Photographs
Cover: Spectrum Colour Library
Benelux Press: 2, 4, 6, 10, 12, 17, 18, 19, 21, 24, 25, 26, 28, 31
Robert Harding Picture Library: 7, 8, 9
Hutchison: 11 (Robert Francis), 14, 29 (P. Goycolea)
Netherlands Board of Tourism: 16, 20, 30, 32
Spectrum Colour Library: 13, 15, 22
Zefa: title page, 3, 5, 23, 27

Library of Congress Cataloging-in-Publication Data: Bailey, Donna. Netherlands/written by Donna Bailey.
p. cm.—(Where we live) Includes index. SUMMARY: Describes life in the busy capital city of Amsterdam,
Holland. ISBN 0-8114-2565-7 1. Netherlands—Social life and customs—Juvenile literature. [1. Netherlands—
Social life and customs. 2. Amsterdam (Netherlands)—Social life and customs.] I. Title. II. Series: Bailey,
Donna. Where we live. DJ71.B27 1991 949.2′352—dc20 91-20188 CIP AC

ISBN 0-8114-2565-7
Copyright 1992 Steck-Vaughn Company
Original copyright Heinemann Children's Reference 1991